IN BROKEN LATIN

In Broken Latin

POEMS BY
ANNETTE SPAULDING-CONVY

The University of Arkansas Press
Fayetteville
2012

ISBN-10: 1-55728-987-5
ISBN-13: 978-1-55728-987-2

16 15 14 13 12   1 2 3 4 5

Designed by Liz Lester

⊗ The paper used in this publication meets the minimum requirements of the American National Standard for Permanence of Paper for Printed Library Materials Z39.48—84.

LIBRARY OF CONGRESS CATALOGING-IN-PUBLICATION DATA

Spaulding-Convy, Annette, 1963–
    In broken Latin : poems / by Annette Spaulding-Convy.
        p.   cm.
    ISBN-13: 978-1-55728-987-2 (pbk. : alk. paper)
    ISBN-10: 1-55728-987-5 (pbk. : alk. paper)
    I. Title.
    PS3619.P3725I5   2012
    811.6—dc23
                                    2012017473

ACKNOWLEDGMENTS

Thanks to the editors of the following journals in which these poems appeared, sometimes in a different form: *Cascade Journal*, "Confessions from an Apiary"; *Crab Creek Review*, "Why She Would Take Off Her Shoes before Jumping From the Golden Gate Bridge"; *Crab Orchard Review*, "An Ex-Nun Resurrects the Dating God"; *In Posse*, "In the Convent We Become Clouds," "There Were No Rules about Underwear"; *Kalliope*, "In the Shower, She Sees White Roses"; *North American Review*, "I bring my newborn to the convent"; *Prairie Schooner*, "Confessions from an Apiary," "Pietà"; and *Spindrift*, "Apologia Pro Vita Mea."

Thanks to the editors of the following anthologies in which these poems appeared, sometimes in a different form: *Northwind Anthology*, "Bonsai Nun," "In the Convent We Become Clouds," "In the Shower, She Sees White Roses," "Lighting Candles to Patsy Cline"; *Pontoon #7: An Anthology of WA State Poets*, "In the Convent We Become Clouds," "In the Shower, She Sees White Roses"; *Pontoon #8: An Anthology of WA State Poets*, "I bring my newborn to the convent," "Lighting Candles to Patsy Cline"; *Pontoon #9: An Anthology of WA State Poets*, "Oratio Nocturna," "There Were No Rules about Underwear"; *Pontoon #10: An Anthology of WA State Poets*, "In the Convent We Become Clouds."

The following poems appeared in my chapbook *In the Convent We Become Clouds*, published by Floating Bridge Press, (Seattle, WA): "After Reciting 333 Titles for The Virgin Mary, I Remember Only 4," "Against the Rules, I've Added Honey to the Altar Bread," "An Ex-Nun Resurrects the Dating God," "Apologia Pro Vita Mea," "Bonsai Nun," "I bring my newborn to the convent," "In the Convent We Become Clouds," "In the Shower She Sees White Roses," "Lighting Candles to Patsy Cline," "Madonna After Vespers (Remix)," "Midnight Snack with Saint Agatha," "Oratio Nocturna," "Pietà," "Saint Valentine's Dinner with Nuns," "There Were No

Rules about Underwear," "Three Classes of Relics," "Virgin Martyrs' Chiffon Dessert," "We Color the White That Binds Us," "Wearing a Scarf of Recycled Sari Yarn, I Want Other Gods," "When the Priest Stays for Sunday Brunch," "You Died before I Sent a Card."

I would like to thank the writers and poets in my writing groups who have been supportive of my work and have so generously offered their feedback on many of these poems: Kelli Russell Agodon, Lana Hechtman Ayers, Ronda Broatch, Nancy Canyon, Jennifer Culkin, Jeannine Hall Gailey, Holly Hughes, Janet Norman Knox, Jenifer Browne Lawrence, and Natasha Kochicheril Moni. This manuscript was completed because of your friendship and encouragement.

Special thanks to the Artist Trust GAP Grant for providing funds for my work.

Thank you to the Sisters of Saint Dominic with whom I was lucky enough to journey for a few years. I learned so much from your exemplary lives of devotion and generosity, commitment to social justice, and passion for the academic life. I would especially like to thank the sisters specifically mentioned in this book, all of whom have passed on: Sister Aquinas Nimitz, Sister Nicholas Maltman, Sister Richard Rhodes, and Sister Samuel Conlan. I'm not sure you would have approved of my poetry, but know that I am forever grateful for the love of ideas, literature, and art that you shared in your classrooms. All of you continue to inspire me.

And very special thanks to my family: Kevin, Selene, and Ian. Thank you for always giving me the time and space to write, edit, and ponder. Thank you for creating a home where I can be crazy and quirky, and still deeply loved.

CONTENTS

I.

After Reciting 333 Titles for The Virgin Mary,
    I Remember Only 4   3

In the Convent We Become Clouds   6

from Uterine Dogma   7

Saint Valentine's Dinner with Nuns   10

Midnight Snack with Saint Agatha   11

There Were No Rules about Underwear   12

Confessions from an Apiary   13

Madonna after Vespers (Remix)   14

Lighting Candles to Patsy Cline   15

Wearing a Scarf of Recycled Sari Yarn,
    I Want Other Gods   16

Against the Rules, I've Added Honey
    to the Altar Bread   17

II.

The Girl with the Tiny Pocketknife   21

Feeding Stations of the Cross   22

Three Classes of Relics   26

Bonsai Nun   27

When the Priest Stays for Sunday Brunch   28

In the Shower, She Sees White Roses   29

Everything except Her Head   30

Sunday Afternoon, Waterboarding   34

III.

Apologia Pro Vita Mea   39

The Morning I Make Vows,
    the Space Shuttle Explodes   41

Pietà   42

Odors of Sanctity   43

The Fleet Admiral's Daughter   45

You Died before I Sent a Card   47

Why She Would Take Off Her Shoes before
    Jumping from the Golden Gate Bridge   49

After the Abortion,
    Summer Visits Me in the Convent   50

Virgin Martyrs' Chiffon Dessert   51

IV.

An Ex-Nun Resurrects the Dating God   55

We Color the White That Binds Us   56

Oratio Nocturna   57

I bring my newborn to the convent   58

"She Got Some Cute Little Lips on Her Wrist"   59

It's Just Hypocrisy Needling Me   61

Six Ways to Sunday   62

Hollow Women   64

Via Negativa   66

Notes   69

I.

Take God for your Spouse and you will never sin.

—SAINT TERESA OF AVILA

I would either have ended up a nun or this.

—MADONNA

After Reciting 333 Titles for The Virgin Mary, I Remember Only 4

I. Unlearned in the Ways of Eve

I wonder if I've entered the convent
because women hold more
mystery than God.

Manless and veiled
they love

with an empathy that's ecstatic
without body or promise.

When I was a postulant,
the Mother Superior called me Mary
Poppins, Little Goody-Two-Shoes.

Sure, I pronounced perfect Latin,
fed the dying Sisters pureed apples

but I still hated my father
and smoked gingseng
cigarettes in the cloister garden.

II. Our Lady of Copacabana

What if I told you that I pray lying
on the black and white tiles of the chapel floor?

What if God's a woman rising from the dirt,
dressed only in a plum, lime, and ruby scarf?

You might call me a heretic.

You might tell the Novice Mistress
jazz and parrots make me blush.

III. Perfume of Faith

Whenever I listen to Schubert's *Ave Maria*
backwards on the record player, I hear

biological clock,   patriarchy

My sister sends a coming out package:

short black skirt
Spice Ice lipstick
Chanel No. 19
tampons

I want to walk out of here
with a snip from each Sister's veil,
my small beliefs
tucked in a pink beaded purse.

IV. Star That Bore the Sea

Some nights it comes into my belly—

a coral uterus the color of angel skin,
and I hold it up in the convent chapel,
    like consecration,
so the Sisters can see the serrated walls.

It's just another organ dream,
the kind you have when your body knows it's finished
    kneeling and confessing, doesn't care
if the congregation knows you have shit to work out before you procreate.

Later when I'm giving birth, I'll bleed volumes
    of the *Summa Theologica*, bleed dogma
from my tear until every red word is gone.

In the Convent We Become Clouds

I lived with women who didn't move
their hips,

but slid like mist
through hallways and chapels,

their curves drowned
in a habit's straight, white sea.

When one of them said,
You walk like a lumberjack,

I wondered why
I hadn't learned to float,

my black pumps
still causing this body to shake

and surface, say *woman*
during silent prayer.

There are things
we can't offer up—

breasts, lips, voice
swung like an ancient ax,

the way we receive communion
on our wet tongues

so that even the oldest priest
will blush.

from Uterine Dogma

Pap

He's wondering whether or not
I'm a virgin,

explains hymens

can break
from horseback riding

or rough insertion

of a tampon.
After signing off
the pre-convent physical,

he rubs my back, tells me
he wants his own daughter

to have a calling.
The dentist will say
the same, brushing his crotch

too close to my cotton-
packed mouth.

Even in a white postulant dress

tiny blood stains from drills and swabs—

even in a white postulant dress.

Prolapse

The old nun will not have the operation.
Forget about prayer or how well she plays Chopin.
Ask why it falls from her as she climbs the oak staircase, why
the intern at the French Hospital tucks it back in with an *en bonne santé!*
while I wait in the lobby, flipping through *Vogue* in my white habit.

Sometimes sacrifice is living without
big hair and red Esprit leggings.
Sometimes sacrifice is staying
intact, in spite of the body slipping
out of itself on this warm piano bench.

Pseudocyesis

Spurious. Feigned. Imaginary.   Hysterical. Phantom. Mental.

Yes, I'm unnerved—
throwing up every morning after mass, the sacrilege of Jesus,
his body and blood communing in my vomitus.

Have you ever felt a nun's swollen breasts?
Peaked at a paunch under yards of white cotton?

I'm thinking there can be no *begetting*
because there hasn't been any *knowing*,
but maybe I've become the parasitic wasp, the fire
ant—a colony of women run amok with asexual reproduction.

Who said *baby fever?*
Who said *I'm not going to pass my crazies to another generation?*

Shh!   I have an urge to eat another jar of peanut butter
behind the statue of the Blessed Virgin Mary.

Bicornuate

What woman wouldn't want a heart
    between her ovaries, a two-chambered
womb with half a wall?

Imagine telling Sexton some of us carry
    almost twice the sweet weight, twenty birds and their thick
wings beating in the space that isn't torn.

Not a birth defect, the Mother Superior tells me.
    A valentine from God delivered in the most intimate
of organs, *So never leave and defile it,*

but even I see it coming: world, men, sex.
    And two children who will remember in which side
of me they grew, what they etched on the pink-laced wall.

Saint Valentine's Dinner with Nuns

In the refectory, I light Sacred Heart
        of Jesus candles, place a neon-pink carnation
    and a Hershey's Kiss on each plate.

My Shirley Temple spiked
        with sacramental wine, I hang a cardboard Cupid
    around Saint Dominic's neck,

then scatter red confetti on the oak table,
        making love
    look like something from a second-grade classroom,

something as virginal as our white dresses.
        For the centerpiece, there's the dime-store
    statue of *The Ecstasy of Saint Teresa,*

that angel jabbing his long spear
        into her breast,
        God's way of saying, *be mine, sweetie-pie,*

luv u, hot stuff—
        Conversation Hearts
    spill like fire into our empty laps.

Midnight Snack with Saint Agatha

I light red votives on the eve of her feast day,
    flip the kneeler up and down with my slipper
until she slides like incense through the sacristy door.

She's not my favorite vision.
    If she would only update herself, lose
the early-middle-ages, poor-me-icon look,

but she sits in the choir stall with a palm branch,
    a silver plate balanced on her knees. At least
she's left the pincers, tongs, knife at home.

I don't like being the patroness of volcanoes,
    she complains, *bread loaves, bells.*
Like a responsorial psalm, I answer:

You're too intense for them,
    carrying your martyred breasts around on a platter;
priests are more comfortable calling them mountains.

She sighs and I offer her some candy—
    white marzipan balls with a dot of pink frosting.
She worries that only the body of Christ should be eaten

    in church, but I tell her it's okay.

There Were No Rules about Underwear

My friend, the Carmelite, could only wear white
       non-bikini panties, laceless bras,

but my order was progressive—red satin, cut
       to show some hip, a midnight-blue Wonderbra

hidden under my habit. The fathers were perceptive, not *priest*
       fathers, but men who flirted with me

while their daughters lit Virgin
       of Guadalupe candles in the chapel alcove,

men like the firefighter, who ran into my bedroom
       the summer night I slept nude, flames

in the cloister attic. I pulled the sheet around my body
       as he looked at black lace on the floor—

I need to feel your walls to see if they're hot.

Confessions from an Apiary

Church candles must contain at least 51 percent (in maxima parte) beeswax, which is Pure, being made by virgin worker bees.

—THE CATHOLIC ENCYCLOPEDIA

If I light one for the Queen
of Heaven, maybe the confession box will drip
with the 49 percent of me that's raw and unfiltered.

Domine, ne despicias me

Through the screen, he looks like a Kitchen God,
his red, paper body hung
above the flames of a thousand busy women.

Quamvis malus, quamvis indignus et peccator

There's always forgiveness for honey in my hip
pocket, for fingers that rub it on his lips.
He'll speak sweetly of me,
explain to the Jade Emperor
why I tumble
into any open flower
when warm days lift me over the threshold.

Illumina me et visita me

One night, I'll burn his paper body like a votive,
catch smoke on my long tongue,
smear the box of matches with nectar.

Madonna after Vespers (Remix)

While the others pause in the alcove
to whisper a prayer to the Virgin,
I go to the recreation room, take off

my black veil and shoes, turn on MTV
as if sipping a martini after work.
I'm not sure why it's refreshing

to watch her grab her own crotch,
cat-lap milk, pour it over her breasts,
then still have energy to seduce a statue

of Jesus, who comes to life
when she kneels in a tight flowered dress.
I want the wood and marble saints

in our chapel to say something, respond
to years of fingered beads—
just one night with Dominic, or better,

Francis, who could teach me Italian,
how to tame feral cats with prosciutto.
While the VJ explains how to pronounce

her last name, *Chee-cone-ay*, I wonder
if I should have been completely cloistered
in a convent where nuns make flavored

honeys, hand-stitch priest stoles, and never read
newspapers. Maybe then I would want to pray
the rosary, not wear it around my hips.

Lighting Candles to Patsy Cline

She's easier than the Virgin—
no flowers, white altar cloths or beads,
just gin neat and a place for her boots by the organ.

I play old records in the chapel at night,
pretend it's a low-lit bar with smoky incense,
my breviary a little black book without any names.

And I've listened to "Crazy" too many times,
every picture of Saint Dominic is the man
who left me for the redhead with breasts,

but I'm married to Jesus now, and special,
even though He sleeps with a thousand brides.

I should make a novena, listen to *Dona Nobis Pacem*,
not want Him to hurt me, give me stigmata
so I can wrap my hands in gauze and forget how to pray.

Wearing a Scarf of Recycled Sari Yarn,
I Want Other Gods

It pours over my white habit
     like a tropical cocktail,
so many lemons, mangos,
even my *mea culpas* are strawberry.

    In the refectory window,
the reflection of my veil
        becomes black hair,
and I touch the extra bead on my rosary,
the vanity I haven't prayed away.

    I will only go so far with Jesus,
won't undress completely,
   like a mistress He visits in another town
who perfumes His tired feet,

    listens to His miracles.
I'm not one of the wives
washing lepers in Calcutta,
raped in El Salvador.

    It's okay being lukewarm.

The morning I met Mother Teresa,
I tried to pull a thread from the blue
    trim of her sari,
and, I swear,
      my hand burned for days.

Against the Rules,
I've Added Honey to the Altar Bread

Saturday afternoon, we're in the confessional.
I'm revealing to you that I've drizzled it
in the bowl between warm water and wheat
flour. What you've been blessing, breaking,
is a sham, an illicit mass.
Maybe I'm trying to tell everyone
flesh can be sweet as spirit.

Remember when Saint Teresa tied
the cilice around her thigh so tight
her skin tore into roses,
and she was disappointed?
And I haven't told you about my sister
who bought a motorcycle on credit
because she didn't want to be *the bitch*
on the back of his bike anymore.
I'm not going to make final vows.

Give me a penance with pizzazz.
Counsel me to hang my habit up,
and I'll shed it here in this dark box,
embarrass you with sounds of my white
bra unclasping, my naked arm reaching
through the screen to feed you panettone—
milk, candied fruit, egg yolks,
your first communion in my savory hand.

II.

My soul takes pleasure from and exults in pain.

—SAINT CATHERINE OF SIENA

Even so, I must admire your skill;
you are so gracefully insane.

—ANNE SEXTON

The Girl with the Tiny Pocketknife

For Kim

*If your hand is your undoing, cut it off; it is better for you to
enter into life maimed than to keep both hands and be cast
into the fires of hell.*

—MARK 9:43

If she had lived back then, she would have watched holy
women scrub themselves with slivers of stained glass, anemic
lips chanting *miserere nobis, Christe eleison* and all that

red, all that red bleeding into white woolen sleeves.
She loves the intensity of ink quills and tacks
from old horseshoes stashed behind the statue of Joseph

the Carpenter, saint of tools with edges. And after evening psalms,
so many candles to pass fingers through, just enough scorch
in the dim chapel to remember flesh. The girl with the tiny pocketknife

knows that carving and burning anarchy symbols into *her* thigh
gets reported, lands *her* butt in therapy, doesn't please Jesus
anymore. But sometimes at night, holy women whisper at her to prick

a little finger, drip three drops of blood on the retro shag rug.
She wishes she knew more Latin, could pray, *I'm opened
now (ego sum aperire nunc?)*, could count in Greek (*ena, dua, tria?*)

the secret ways to saint herself with this hot-pink blade.

Feeding Stations of the Cross

I.

I consider mailing cottage cheese and grape jello
to starving children in Vietnam. Slap me
again for every forkful uneaten at supper, guilty
vinyl ripping beneath these beanpole legs.

II.

If I pray to Clare of Pisa to disappear
my waist, maybe she'll load my sheepish bra
with a handful of extra flesh. I'd carry it well.

III.

Pope Lady Buns

Scald milk and sugar
Add yeast, flour until soft
Punch down
Cut into ladies
Poke in currants for eyes
Let rise

IV.

While my mother listens to Patsy Cline and Mother Maybelle Carter,
my father screws her blonde friend in the blue trailer.
Later, she'll pop a sugar-free Fresca, pour it over ice
cream, ask me if I see his pickup swaggering down the road.

V.

Some days when I drink only lemon juice and water,
there are seagulls crying in the pipes of the church
organ, a raven-black priest feeding me a suet wafer.

VI.

And some days when I faint, a fat nun finds a crumb
of doughnut on her kneeler, tucks it zealously under my tongue.

VII.

Dry Bones Cookies

Cream sugar, butter, nutmeg until light and airy
Sprinkle with rosewater
Roll into little femurs, fibulae, and clavicles
Bake until rock hard

VIII.

I'm just beginning to locate
my soul, and look, I've forgotten to fast!
Coffee with cream, raisin cinnamon roll,
the other nuns drinking weak tea on this sad, sad Friday.

IX.

Virgin Dinner Knots

Dissolve yeast in warm water
Stir in milk, eggs, flour
Beat

Let rest
Tie into small tight knots

X.

Whenever I kneel, I think of my body as a window, my white habit
a curtain covering the view—ample grass, a gangly
rockrose, the swing set rusting, childless.

XI.

My body is a window. The stupid jay stuns itself
against me, reflection of mustard seed spilled across a kitchen table.

XII.

What is God? I ask
my dead father in a dream. He hands me a sirloin
steak, shrink wrapped in Styrofoam—enigmatic
bastard.

XIII.

I'm sick
of talking to dead people
and the dead are tired
of listening to me unload
my grocery sacks
of affliction.

XIV.

Tell me again that it's sexy to see a woman
eat, sexy when she slurps mussels like a seal, weighty
and lean as a spoonful of salted ocean.

Three Classes of Relics

I.

It's a form of prayer to cut a woman's body
into pieces—
a veiled head sent to Rome, a little finger to Amiens,
bones broken and shared as though they were bread.

I stood in line once to see Saint Clare's heart.
Her pulmonary veins had crisscrossed into words,
and I thought I could make out *amore* on the left
ventricle, which must have pulsed hot
pink when she was alive, a valentine from God.

II.

They probably fought over the corset. Her hairbrush,
the board she used to knead dough each morning,
even the sheets were given to her family,
but the corset rested on her ribs, opened like a door.

III.

If I could have broken the glass case,
I might have touched a pen to her heart
then written words red and wet as apples

or taken off my black stockings, held them to *amore*
and put them back on, my varicose veins
spelling the places where I've stood too long.

Bonsai Nun

It can happen when a god loves
    you too much. He answers prayers
        with a simple slate tray,
            a pair of *jin* pliers, then whispers
                something about sweet curvature
of soul. What you take for love
pinches is really his tiny pruning
of everything that might end
in a forked twig or red fruit.
    Ask Eve. She'll tell you about life
        after the fiasco
            when Adam wouldn't stop
                obsessing over the tree,
                    how he gave her wire, a trunk
                    splitter, wanted her body
            a semi-cascade
        in a glazed *Tokoname* pot.
      Most gods don't crave
      an elongated neck,
      stunted feet; they want
      a certain bend
    as you kneel on your *prie-dieu.*
They count your leaves like a rosary,
say *mmm* gazing on your arch-like ribs.
Ask Eve about the scoliosis and the osteoporosis.
She'll tell you she's glad she can't look at the sky;
the ripest apples for pie are always somewhere in the dirt.

When the Priest Stays for Sunday Brunch

They look like Our Lady
    of the Snows or Grace

Kelly, white flowers held
    in a wimple's stiff vase.

In aprons they pour tea,
    bring Tabasco for his eggs—

priest servers caught
    between the prayers

of their slender hands.

    And the dish washers,

too plump and red cheeked
    for the dining room, think

of Saint Rose scrubbing herself
    with lye and habaneros

when the men of Lima
    eyed her during church—

so many vain petals
    swallowed in a hungry sink.

In the Shower, She Sees White Roses

A wet thigh, neck, soapy red hair,

she finds her body here—
places she can't even name anymore,
her veil and scapular draped over the toilet.

She would die for a full-length mirror
to see if her butt is really as big as it feels,
if fasting cures more than just the soul.

Saint Catherine did it well,
years of communion wafers and water,
bedridden, but holy and lean.

And Catherine got something else—
four hours of ecstatic union with God,
who must have been pleased by what He saw,

a woman dying to be with Him.
When hot water hits the curve of her back,
sometimes flowers rise from porcelain tiles,

and she wonders if He is here—
a bouquet or at least a corsage
to pin on her small breast.

Everything except Her Head

*His Eminence, German Cardinal Joseph Ratzinger is
meeting with us tonight in the Commons to assess our
compliance with the Vatican's "male only" seminary
guidelines. We request that our female students, given
the nature of his visit, not attend, but assist "behind the
scenes" with the preparation of desserts and cocktails.*

—THEOLOGY SCHOOL BULLETIN

I. Dogmatic Ramifications of Piping Bittersweet Chocolate into "Christ's Diaper" Lenten Cookies

Sometimes when a woman is cutting
pastry dough into small triangles
she's not thinking of the Trinity—

father   son   holyspirit
but the pink symbol on the bumper
of her lesbian neighbor's Subaru.

It happens once or twice,
an epiphany of shapes and why
the right angle of her soul

always points to the broken kitchen
chair. Sometimes when a woman is shaving
dark chocolate into a double-boiler,

she's not thinking of bitterness,
but whether she would ever pierce
her labia.   Ruby?   Diamond?

Ruby.   Definitely   bloodredruby.

II. Severed Hagiography: Lesson Plan

+ Saint Catherine
  - ✓ torso in Rome
  - ✓ foot in Venice
  - ✓ head in Siena

Student Reflection Question: *Has your whole sadness ever knotted
into a quiet ovary, bleeding one month and not the next?*

+ Mother Cabrini
  - ✓ torso in New York
  - ✓ hands in San Angelo
  - ✓ head in San Angelo

Student Reflection Question: *Have you smelled the fragile white
rage of certain lilies?*

+ Saint Elizabeth
  - ✓ torso in Marburg
  - ✓ rib in Vienna
  - ✓ head in Vienna

Student Reflection Question: *You considered using a penknife
as a means of personal devotion,*

didn't you?

III. Cocktail Exegesis:
A Slow Comfortable Screw Against The Wall

She's tired of explaining
to the German cardinal in red shoes why
she keeps forgetting the Galliano

in his drink. Doesn't he know the world
has enough walls and maybe all we need
to swallow is a Slow Comfortable Screw?

She could give a homily
on sloe gin, Southern Comfort, a juiced
orange, and the chaffing from too many tips

tucked in her bra at two a.m., but
the German cardinal in red shoes
doesn't want to discuss sore breasts

and, frankly, she's not ready to confess.
She may or may not explain
the thin girl doing shots of altar wine,

lighting Virginia Slims with a white votive.

IV. Severed Hagiography: Student Answers/Assessment

✓ *No, my fractured sadness is trying to translate, I bleed*
every month into Hebrew, Greek and Aramaic.

✓ *Yes, desperate pollen always finds another calla*
lily, hiding the swollen pink of her stigma.

✓ *Maybe I'm a cutter. Maybe I don't eat for days.*
Don't misunderstand—my devotion

is wide open.

Sunday Afternoon, Waterboarding

We do not torture.

> —GEORGE W. BUSH, defending US interrogation
> practices in CIA prisons overseas

I'm not thinking sports here, surf and boogie, beach blanket
    bingo or Frankie Avalon
bedding someone in the perfect sand, but I'm thinking strapped
naked to a plank and dunked in a tub until you black
    out. I'm saying don't worry,

you'll be resuscitated with little or no lung damage, maybe
    a smidgen of oxygen
brain deprivation so they can collect some information
    that will save us all,

amen. Thank God, when I was in the convent, they didn't think
of us as witches, but I thought of us as witches, white
    for sure, praying
spells for my mother's elaborate tumor, tarot cards
    veiled under my black

veil in the closet since my life was all cups—blood, water, wine.
    I was taught to hold everything
in my nun's big-mother heart. Lord knows, if there's any martyring
to be done, call the nuns who bled themselves on the nuclear silo

and ended up in jail with Martha Stewart, not so much for bleeding
    as cutting
the military's metal fence, an offense as big as national defense.
I'm saying don't worry, we're not Salem or the Middle Ages—

we'd never let a waterboarded Martha come home to Turkey
    Hill, Connecticut, too terrified to sip
Perrier, scared so silly she can't cut parsley when it rains.

III.

I feel nothing but joy at the thought of death.

—SAINT THÉRÈSE OF LISIEUX

Dying
Is an art, like everything else.
I do it exceptionally well. . . .

I guess you could say I've a call.

—SYLVIA PLATH

Apologia Pro Vita Mea

In Memory of Sister Richard

You keep dying—

another brittle limb
near the center of the cloister garden
falls in slow time
from the weary eucalyptus.

I can't be there now
stammering off key
while you sing the *Salve Regina*
perfectly in four parts,
a coffin
again borne with grace
down the front stairs of the motherhouse.

I try not to think of it
as failure,
the way so many of us
vowed, then left,
the way I promised you
I would be an earthen vessel
holding and handing down
your passion for books.

In springtime in the chapel,
pink-orange quince blossoms

on the altar, you make ready
another burial,
and learning of it weeks later,
I find her copies
of Virgil and Horace
yellowed without thought
on my shelf.

And knowing I did with my life
the only thing I could do,
I ask some sort of absolution
from her in broken Latin.

The Morning I Make Vows,
the Space Shuttle Explodes

Jan. 28, 1986

In one story, a woman is stitching skies
full of red bats on a silk robe.

She slips her hand into a pocket,
says, *Emptiness is the place between stars*

where heaven is born.
Later, she will watch fireworks

fall into a lake—
Chrysanthemum Shower, Dancing Peony.

In another story, a woman leaves
her bed to see the *Tears of Saint Lawrence*

drop behind the chapel spire.
On nights the sky weeps

dust, she wishes for an umbrella
sewn from pages of hymns,

Panis Angelicus opened over her head
to catch a tired universe.

Pietà

For Josephine Convy

It's the virgin's hemline she remembers
and a wedge of *parmigiano*
dunked in balsamic vinegar so red

she thinks of blood or maybe chianti.
In the catacombs it's wine, a mossy
bone smell like crushed grapes,

but she comes back to the lace
on the edge of the dress.
She could count every stitch—

honeycomb, open-fan, rose, heart,
a litany of virgin names softer
than any thread spun from stone.

She doesn't speak of the dying
man's weight or the folds
where the dress is a cradle,

but of the virgin's height if she could rise—
seven feet and lace
dripping over those sandals like honey.

Odors of Sanctity

Imagine buying the smell of Jesus Christ in a jar—it's for sale. Now you can experience His smell, thanks to a couple in South Dakota. Their candle is based on the 45th Psalm, "Your robes are fragrant with myrrh and aloes and cassia."

—CBS NEWS

I.

He doesn't want to be remembered
like a lesson from *Culpepper's Herbal.*

If it were up to Him, He'd take beeswax,
mix in vinegar, sweat, olive wood,

include instructions to let the match burn
to thumb and forefinger before lighting—

even a little pain teases death,
and God knows, He still dreams

of that afternoon, how surprising it was
to feel His lungs drowning in so much air.

II.

Someone told me,
People die the way they live,

so when we found her in the convent
bathroom in a stall of her own blood,

I thought it was appropriate,
one of her vows being privacy.

After I tossed the rags, put away
the Lysol, I couldn't get death

out of my nose for days.
I stole Easter incense from the chapel,

burned it—aromatherapy
until my lungs opened like lilies.

III.

The Irish Sisters say he was shot
because he was Catholic,

hang his portrait in the refectory
next to Mother McAuley.

He watches them, *in perpetuum*,
eat broiled tomatoes and blood sausage.

Sometimes in late November,
they light votives on linen placemats—

spiced cranberry with a hint of limousine
exhaust, brain, and Jackie's Chanel.

The Fleet Admiral's Daughter

For Sister Aquinas Nimitz

I. Nuclear Powered US Aircraft Carrier, Class Name: Nimitz

I think of your life as a tide pool—
filled, emptied twice a day, morning and evening

psalms, the red anemone of your soul anchored to this choir stall.
Sometimes you found your name deployed in the Arabian Sea

or Persian Gulf, so you walked the beach in your habit and black cape,
draped seaweed over urchins, gulls dive-bombing them at low tide.

And thank you for not making a show of it,
like Sarah Winchester, who built a thousand rooms to wall

out a thousand Civil War ghosts, shot with the family gun.
Did you ever pray to the sea, pray

to the sea, *ad nauseum*, until it re-christened you—
salt water breaking against the sharp fin of your ankles?

II. Litania Humilitas Mortuorum

Mystical Marine Biologist,   *pray for us.*

Teacher in the Chloroform-Stained Habit,   *pray for us.*

Joyful Conchologist,   *pray for us.*

Sister Advocate of Peace,   *pray for us.*

Quiet Carrier of the Cancerous Cells,   *pray for us.*

III. Sunburst Carrier Shell, Class Name: Gastropoda

The first time we shelled Baghdad, you were pruning
roses before evening prayer and when a student yelled,

It's on TV; it looks like fireworks!

you left the bush, dead stems still hanging.
I watched you amble toward the convent chapel

so weighted and worried, you reminded me
of the small mollusk who cements so much sea

debris to her shell, she sinks in the tropical silt.
You anchored yourself to that choir stall, praying

Our Father on a string of knotted kelp.

You Died before I Sent a Card

For Sister Samuel

You always warned me
       about procrastination,
but a late term paper on John Donne's compass
conceit wasn't death,
           even though you commented,
Your romanticism clouds the water of metaphysical poetry.

Did you know at age forty, I still wrote
      two rough drafts
for every letter I sent you?
You might have enjoyed the card:

thnx for the tea when i came to shakespeare
class early drunk

I think about your dislike of *foolish consistency,*
little minds (Emerson?) and how you moved
          tradition like a stone,

so I don't imagine you in heaven,
but you're riding that damn compass
             at a carnival, hanging on
to the sweeping arm
looking as you did before the convent,
      Katharine Hepburn with red hair.

And you flirt with the man making cotton candy,
feel the pocket of your denim capris for a dime
while he swirls sugar in a perfect circle.
                You wonder, *Is he God?*

Why She Would Take Off Her Shoes
before Jumping from the Golden Gate Bridge

Maybe the water
is a temple

and white boats below
so many devotees

pointing
where to lay down

the orchid of herself,
incense burning

like salt.
She doesn't want

to bring the road's dirt
inside,

but unbuckles on the step
and tears open

the soft door,
floating gulls screaming

like angels.

After the Abortion,
Summer Visits Me in the Convent

She's come here to spread tarot cards across an oak pew.
Sometimes this is what it takes to figure out
if it was the guy who beaded her white Virgo bracelet
or the classical guitarist at the Spanish Bistro.

Sometimes this is what it takes to figure out
why a woman craves absolution from a woman, forgiveness
because the aching guitarist at the Spanish Bistro
left a blood-red rose in her flamenco sheets.

She craves a woman's absolution from me, forgiveness
with the laying on of my nun hands
for the flamenco-red blood she left on the clinic sheets,
a *Dios te salve Maria* under a frosted glass window.

With the laying on of my hands
this is how we pray, amethyst crystal on her breast,
a *Dios te salve Maria* under the stained glass window.
Somewhere between San Francisco and Barcelona

she prays, amethyst crystal on her breast,
tarot cards spread across an oak pew
somewhere between San Francisco and Barcelona
she's fingering milk-white beads on a Virgo bracelet.

Virgin Martyrs' Chiffon Dessert

Begin by cutting, no, *crushing*
    the strawberries, then whip
        evaporated milk, rest
    in boiling water over high flame.

I haven't made this in years,
    haven't thought about iconography
        in the convent kitchen—
    Cecilia, Agnes, Ursula

hanging over the microwave,
    examples of how to lay
        down our lives over lentil soup.
    It's not that I wanted to die,

but I wasn't afraid of it then,
    could picture myself stiff
        in a clean, white habit
    while mourners ate funeral

cookies, drank fruit punch.
    When I heard about the nun,
        her face shot three times
    in the Brazilian rainforest,

I thought of crushed berries,
    the way celibacy blooms love
        like yeast in warm water.
    Is this why there's no dessert

for *mother* martyrs—
    because we won't die
        for trees or gods, our lives bound
    here by a blood-stained cord?

IV.

The soul is kissed by God in its innermost regions.
—BLESSED HILDEGARD VON BINGEN

I used to be Snow White, but I drifted.
—MAE WEST

An Ex-Nun Resurrects the Dating God

They give me white roses, never red, and cards
    with old Sisters on merry-go-rounds. They tell me
        their mothers light Virgin of Guadeloupe
    candles, thankful that I'm a *nice* girl.

I answer their convent curiosity:
    No, there wasn't a tunnel to the priest's rectory.
        A few lesbians, but most were asexual.
    Not just tea, we had a liquor cabinet.

They confess ex-girlfriends who taught tantric
    yoga, something about legs, incense, orgasms
        of the spirit. They think I'm Our Lady of Lourdes,
    my water washes memory.

I should say I'm nobody's salvation, I've stopped
    carrying crosses, rolling away the stone,
        but I might show them the medal of Saint Anne
    sewn into the left cup of my old bra.

They'd rather enshrine me, sleep
    with other women because they're afraid
        I'll break. They want me to cook in a black veil—
    lasagna followed by the rosary.

I want the body of Christ
    on my tongue, not the white wafer,
        but bread made of dark honey, whole wheat,
    the way earth would taste if it were flesh.

We Color the White That Binds Us

I find my old habit in the back of the closet,
black veil folded in a bottom drawer,
and I think of Frida Kahlo painting thorns
on her plaster corset, drips of *raw sienna*
laced across her broken spine.

It's not about pain, but how we're molded
to its form. Hardened into prayer, I walked
without bending, a porcelain doll,
habit hung every night near the crucifix
where Christ could see the hem beginning to fray.

Maybe on the back, I'll sketch a rib
returning to man because it's tired
of the story—woman should have been born
from a slice of apple, the kind with pink
flesh that doesn't bruise.

Should I paint breasts on the front?
They're clay-brown and sag to the belly.
Having fed no one, they've fed everyone, a Zen koan.

And last, I'll dunk the brush in *cadmium red deep,*
splash it like rubied holy water
because we can never bleed enough for Diego
or Jesus, never undress all the way
without them wanting to touch our scars.

Oratio Nocturna

When the dead come to us in our bedroom,
I wait as they say the last psalm

of Compline before asking them to leave.
I apologize to you for bringing them here,

for bringing them into every place we've lived,
but intercession is like a silver thread

tied between my tongue and eternity,
a thousand rosaries to keep these women

praying around us, so I won't forget
the sound of Latin or the taste of faith.

I've told you my ghost stories—
a glimpse of Sister David near the chapel,

Sister Natalie in the cloister garden, and now,
even you seem thankful when the bedroom

fills at night, pages turned in old breviaries,
making love to Gregorian Chant.

I bring my newborn to the convent

and worry she will spit-up peaches
                on their white dresses,
but they press her to their chests, sing psalms
                in Latin, a celibate lullaby.

I left god here
                in a stained glass window
when I packed my vows, blamed everything
on the Annunciation, sun crossing its panels
                like jade.

They ask me what it's like to give birth,
so I talk blood, stitches, how my body
                was an hourglass
spilling sand and constellations all night.
One of them says when she had a hysterectomy,

her twin was found in her uterus, a tumor
                of little bones, teeth, hair,
and I wonder if this is how Mary felt,
                a stone in her pocket,
no stars, no lover, just heavy desert.

"She Got Some Cute Little Lips on Her Wrist"

*Britney Spears's tattoo artist Max Gott, talking to Fox
News after Spears shaves her head, tattoos her wrist, and
checks in to detox.*

Her day could be called postpartum, monastic.

I've been there—
shorn head, no makeup,
ash gray sweatshirt with a hood,
nail stuck in the skin, dead
drunk from too much altar wine.

Tell me the difference between *Body & Soul
Tattoos* in West L.A. and *Convent of the Five Wounds* outside Lodi.

I'm guessing it was a sinkhole beneath her sternum,
the soft-boiled doldrums that stay
up until dawn trying to alphabetize things without names.

At *Convent of the Five Wounds* outside Lodi
we called it *dark night of the soul*, zenemptiness,
when the four-chambered heart is so hollow
even blood can see its own shadow.

There, depression is holy.
There, I watched snowy egrets stand on one leg in the delta for hours,
no one bawling in the background for breast milk or sex.

I admit I prayed once
for stigmata, just a penny-nail hole in my lower palm, red

as a cinnamon candy. It never happened
because my desolation didn't have enough oomph.

At *Body & Soul Tattoos* in West L.A.
she drank some caramel appletinis while he poked her
skin above the radial artery with cherry-colored dye.
Maybe she thought the ink drills were hummingbirds

and these new lips might say something sweet:
No, there's not a paunch between the pink cami and your jeans.
No, the razor cut on your scalp doesn't mean your life is fucked.

It's Just Hypocrisy Needling Me

For thirty-three nights I vigiled outside San Quentin,
cupping white votive candles for death
row inmates because Jesus wouldn't kill
anyone, not even the hypothetical rapist raping
His hypothetical daughter on the desert's edge.

And one morning I protested on a rock outside
the Nevada Test Site, arms linked with other Sisters,
our veils wind lifted, one black banner
sucking in sun and collateral radiation.

Now, I'm remembering the June I stopped being a nun.
I'm remembering the May I started having babies.
Maybe it's spring that makes me harsh, nursing
cracked nipples, vaginal stitches, those Amnesty
International letters tossed in the recycle bin.

Where is that life I built from altar rails and pale wafers,
the spouseless, childless pew from which I loved
everyone so cleanly, a sort of scoured compassion?

Just today, I find myself worrying about squirrels
hawk hunted in my yard, but hating the hypothetical
forty-something sex-offender down the road
eyeballing my daughter as she walks to school.

So what if he's living with his mother because she's on chemo.
So what if the sand a thousand miles away keeps exploding.

Six Ways to Sunday

I.

I arrange my spices the way my mother arranged her medicine cabinet—

ginger, cumin, cardamom, cinnamon, mace, basil

Valium, Librium, Pepto-Bismol, Nembutal, Noxzema, Bayer.

It's not about compulsion, but the *ordo divinus* of things, why

ginger can never be near basil (the cake will fall

today) nor Valium next to Bayer (how easily the irrational rises).

II.

In the Litany Of Our Lady Of Seven Sorrows, *pray for us*
is repeated forty-seven times, *mother* sixteen, and *love* isn't

said at all. Sometimes when I try to make laundry
contemplative and monastic, I sort seven piles of dirty

clothes, name them after the sacraments: panties of confession, flannel
sheets of matrimony, shit-stained diapers of extreme unction . . .

III.

Like a good mother, I check the iron
check the iron to be sure the red dial is pointing *Off*
check the iron every twelve minutes for two hours

like a good mother, I would never want to be seen
running from a burning house or toward one,
the *flamma Dei* licking at these postpartum thighs.

IV.

Don't laugh at me because I hoard muffins
bought in boxes of twenty-four from Costco and Wal-Mart
in case of earthquake or terrorism or sudden
guests. Remember the old nun who stashed biscuits in the chapel?

Her family hid a Jewish woman in the attic for three years.
The thing is, some of us know the situation is already grave.

V.

I'm fumbling through the soul's lexicon, looking up
ways to shut down my ten thousand blasphemous thoughts:
Edit, Replace, Find What <*existential emptiness*> <*cosmological myth*>
Replace With <*purple finch*> <*flowering plum*>
And what if I drink too much beer and smoke a clove cigarette?

Insert <*goji berries, raw almonds, maybe some edamame*>

VI.

Today, Bayer is next to Valium (how easily the irrational rises)
and basil's near the ginger (the cake will fall).
It's not about obsession, but the *ordo divinus* of things:
Bayer, Noxzema, Nembutal, Pepto-Bismol, Librium, Valium
basil, mace, cinnamon, cardamom, cumin, ginger—
my mother arranged her medicine cabinet the way I arrange my spices.

Hollow Women

*My smile is a cloak that covers everything. I speak as if
my very heart is in love with God. What hypocrisy.*
—FROM THE LETTERS OF MOTHER TERESA

Don't feel sorry for us, medicate
us, don't meditate on us with rainbow energy.

       Don't call child protective services, assume
       my husband isn't getting any, don't
       bring me a week's worth of zucchini lasagna.

Believe me, I keep discovering my house
is not a convent and this kitchen not a chapel.
There isn't a room where the paring-knife hole
in my side can bleed its nothing, bleed
its nothing without interruption.

       Just give me Halloween—
       one black and white nun costume to trick
       even Jesus, a loaf of *pan de muerto*
       to feed the thin cratered moon.

Give me All Hallows' Eve—
an orange vegetable metaphor with a silver
spoon. Scooped and emptied, I'm wrapping
every damn seed that tangles me
in yesterday's newspaper, chicken feed.

So let me mourn when nobody's died.
I swear it's less like navel-gazing and more like the black
hole of my gut, my white cell Pleiades
spinning in the part of the painting the artist leaves blank.

And don't let hollow women burn
their brooding letters like straw.
Remind them sometimes even saints suck

    it up, grin, summon
    grace from a god-empty breast.

Via Negativa

I said to my soul, be still, and let the dark come upon you
Which shall be the darkness of God.
                    —T. S. ELIOT, FROM *FOUR QUARTETS*

At some point, you put the *Letters of Mother*
Teresa down, look through piles of papers for the photo
of you in your habit, *Novice '86* written on the back.

You find the black veil in a drawer and drape it
over your head, and soon he will walk into the bedroom
and ask, *Why are you doing this again?*

And you'll say, *It's too sunny outside.*
Forget that you live so far north everything's in shadow,
you're remembering another sun.

All day you've waited for fog,
and when it finally rolled in, you'd fallen asleep.
Even in your sleep someone had left a light on.

So what if he's still standing in the doorway,
you primp your black veil in the mirror
because you need the darkness you haven't had since *novice,*

when you sat two days under an orange tree in the convent
garden because Sister Nicholas dropped dead from a coronary
after teaching Chaucer's "Second Nun's Tale."

Do you remember crying for her like the ringed-bill gull?

How many oranges can a young nun peel in two days?

Somewhere between the Angelus bell and three Tylenol,
there were voices in Middle English:
The droghte of March hath perced to the roote,

and you stopped kneeling, let go your medieval bones.

You pick up *Mother Teresa* again and remind yourself
Mother Teresa slept alone on a straw mat in the middle
of Calcutta. She wanted to torch her own letters

so that Calcutta wouldn't know she had the longest *dark night*
of the soul on spiritual record. Sometimes you wish everyone
were an ex-nun or ex-monk, so that on the city bus you could shoot

the breeze about your soul's aridity and everyone would know
what you meant. No one would worry
because you haven't picked up the phone in a week.

You'll wear your black veil until the dinner dishes
are soaped and clean, potato peels, drumsticks thrown
to the raccoons, one barred owl chanting a shrill psalm.

NOTES

After Reciting 333 Titles for The Virgin Mary, I Remember Only 4

The *Summa Theologica*, written by Saint Thomas Aquinas, is a compilation of the Roman Catholic Church's theological teachings from the church's inception to the thirteenth century.

Midnight Snack with Saint Agatha

Minne De Vergine, "Breasts of the Virgin," are round, white marzipan candies with a pink dot on top, made in celebration of Saint Agatha's feast day by a group of Sicilian nuns to commemorate her martyrdom.

Confessions from an Apiary

Domine, ne despicias me is Latin for "Lord, don't despise me." *Quamvis malus, quamvis indignus et peccator* is Latin for "Ever so bad, ever so unworthy and a sinner." *Illumina me et visita me* is Latin for "Enlighten me and come to me."

Lighting Candles to Patsy Cline

Dona Nobis Pacem is Latin for "Grant us peace" and is a traditional Catholic hymn.

Wearing a Scarf of Recycled Sari Yarn, I Want Other Gods

Mea culpa is Latin for "my fault." Maryknoll nuns Maura Clarke and Ita Ford, Ursuline nun Dorothy Kazel, and Catholic lay worker Jean Donovan were raped and murdered in El Salvador in 1980.

Against the Rules, I've Added Honey to the Altar Bread

A *cilice* is both a hairshirt and a spiked metal belt worn around the upper thigh to mortify the flesh. Panettone is an Italian fruitcake with the texture of light bread.

The Girl with the Tiny Pocketknife

Miserere nobis is Latin for "Have mercy on us" and *Christe eleison* is Greek for "Christ have mercy."

Feeding Stations of the Cross

The poem is based on the fourteen Stations of the Cross, a devotion commemorating the final hours of Jesus's life:

> Jesus is condemned
> The cross is laid upon him
> His first fall
> He meets his Mother
> Simon of Cyrene helps him
> His face is wiped by Veronica
> His second fall
> He meets the weeping women of Jerusalem
> His third fall
> He is stripped of his garments
> His crucifixion
> His death on the cross
> His body is taken down from the cross
> He is placed in the tomb

Three Classes of Relics

The relics of a saint as defined by the Roman Catholic Church:

> First-Class Relic: the body or body parts of a saint.

Second-Class Relic: any personal items used by the saint.

Third-Class Relic: an item that has touched either a first-class relic or a second-class relic.

Everything except Her Head

Cardinal Joseph Ratzinger was elected Pope Benedict XVI in April 2005. As a cardinal, Joseph Ratzinger was Prefect for the Congregation of the Doctrine of the Faith, the group safeguarding the teachings of the Roman Catholic Church and previously known as the Holy Office of the Inquisition.

Sunday Afternoon, Waterboarding

Waterboarding is a form of torture dating from the Inquisition. The victim is repeatedly drowned and resuscitated. "The nuns who bled themselves on a nuclear silo" refers to the three Dominican nuns (Ardeth Platte, Jackie Hudson, and Carol Gilbert) who were arrested for interfering with the national defense by pouring their own blood at a Minuteman III missile silo in Colorado in October 2002.

Apologia Pro Vita Mea

The title of this poem is Latin for "An Apology For My Own Life." *Salve Regina* is Latin for "Hail, Holy Queen" and is a traditional Catholic hymn.

The Morning I Make Vows, the Space Shuttle Explodes

The space shuttle *Challenger* exploded after takeoff on January 28, 1986, killing all seven crewmembers. The Tears of Saint Lawrence is another name for the Perseid meteor shower, which occurs yearly in August near the feast day of Saint Lawrence, martyred by being burned alive. *Panis Angelicus* (a traditional Latin hymn) is translated "Bread of Angels."

The Fleet Admiral's Daughter

Litania Humilitas Mortuorum is Latin for "Humble Litany of the Dead."

After the Abortion, Summer Visits Me in the Convent

Dios te salve Maria is Spanish for "Hail Mary."

Virgin Martyrs' Chiffon Dessert

This poem is dedicated to Sister Dorothy Stang, the seventy-four-year-old Dominican nun and environmentalist murdered in Brazil in February 2005.

Oratio Nocturna

The title of this poem is Latin for "Night Prayer." *Compline* is the last set of monastic prayers recited at night.

Six Ways to Sunday

Ordo divinus is Latin for "divine order" and *flamma Dei* is Latin for "flame of God." Extreme Unction is the traditional name of the Catholic sacrament also known as Anointing of the Sick or Last Rites.

Hollow Women

Pan De Muerto, "bread of the dead" is baked to celebrate Mexico's Day of the Dead on November 2.

Via Negativa

The title of this poem is Latin for "The Negative Way" and refers to the theology that God can only be described by what God is not rather than what God is.